## LES BAUX-DE-PROVENCE

© ÉDITIONS ÉQUINOXE
Domaine de Fontgisclar, Draille de Magne
13570 Barbentane

ISBN 2-84135-229-3
ISSN 1276-4416

# *Vegetable dishes*

## *from l'Oustau de Baumanière*

### Jean-André Charial

*Illustrations by Lizzie Napoli*

TRANSLATION BY JULIE ROSSINI

MAKING UP AND TYPOGRAPHY BY GILLES ALLAIN

ÉQUiN•XE

# Introduction

*Why a cookbook exclusively constituted
of vegetable recipes ?*

*In 1985, I had a fabulous trip to India, where not only did
I discover the magic of this country and its culture, but
also the diversity and the variety of its vegetarian cuisine.*

*Everyday, we would be invited to the table of families
who did not eat fish or meat, and leaving without feeling
ravenous opened up entirely new horizons for me.*

*At the same time, my grandfather Raymond Thuilier,
founder of l'Oustau de Baumanière, started to grow peas
and beans in a garden near la Cabro d'Or. The quality of
the vegetables we gathered was incomparable. First because of their freshness, as they are gathered in the morning,*

and cooked that very same day. Second, because they are gathered when they are still very small.

This is when I realised that luxury was not about serving caviar or foie gras, but about serving very fresh vegetables, gathered and prepared on the same day.

I then decided to bring on the "carte" a set menu constituted of vegetable dishes only. We have now been offering our vegetable menus through changes and seasons for almost fifteen years.

This book is the result of our work during these years. Vegetables are seldom highlighted as they should be, as cleaning and preparing them takes time, and other quick preparations are often preferred to them nowadays.

I think it is a pity, and I hope this book makes you want to bring them frequently on your table for the ones you love.

*The Baux de Provence.*

# OUSTAU DE BAUMANIÈRE

The visitor is first of all struck by the imposing aspect of the place (but then the poet Dante did come through here, so perhaps it's not surprising).

Then there's the warmth of the welcome: as if they'd been expecting your arrival all their lives.

Just let yourself float along; your hosts will take care of everything. Even your travel-crumpled clothes will come back as fresh as new, neatly laid out in a basket.

You will have to make a feww choices at the restaurant, however. From a range of dishes you may never have heard of before; all of them delicious.

*The restaurant.*

One of the gardens that your room or suite will look out onto. Why not wander down to have breakfast in the open air?

*The terrace of the manor house.*

This big terrace above the Baumanière restaurant.
You can stretch out here on cruise liner-style
deckchairs, and tan while admiring the landscape.

The interior dining-room. Its vaulted
stone ceiling is perfect for the cool of the evening,
while in winter the chandeliers and a roaring wood
blaze in the high fireplace are a satisfactory
substitute for the sun.

Why not throw a party? A gourmet caterer is at
your disposal.

*At the entrance to the manor house, one of the houses that make up the hotel.*

In the gardens.

In hall the rooms and
on all the tables you'll
find bunches of wild
Provencal flowers and plants.
plants. Jerome, the local
flower-merchant, picks these
fragrant treasures in the local hills.

The "cabro d'or", fountain.

*La Guigou, another house.*

*A bedroom in an apartment that looks out onto a magnificent garden, and across the whole valley.*

*The boutique.*

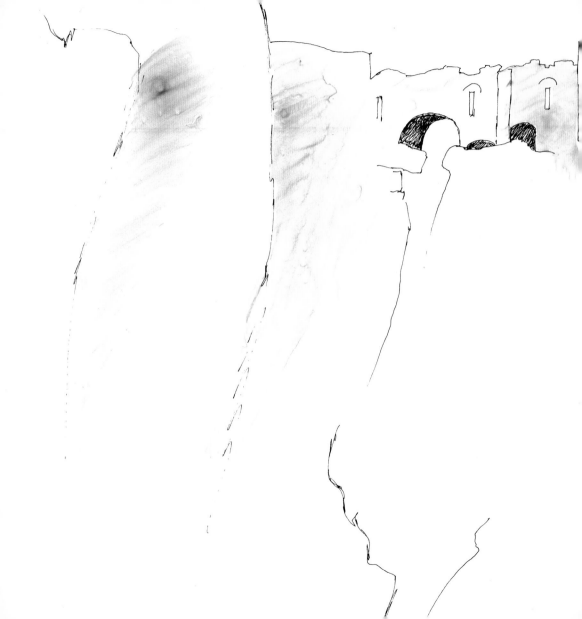

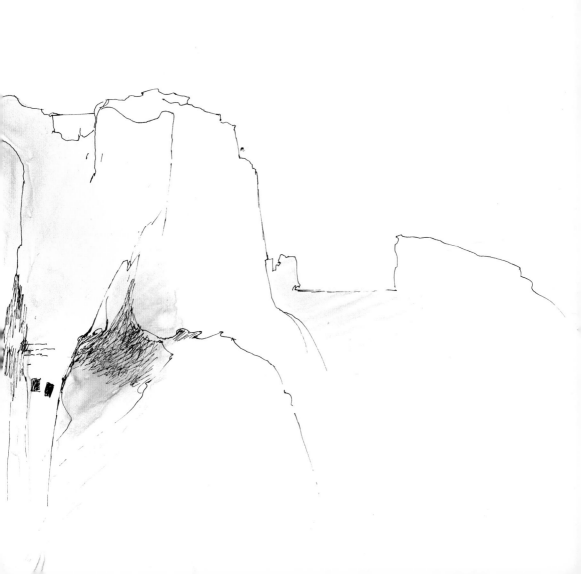

## Menu

### SOUPS Soupes, potages et veloutés

Crème de chou-fleur à l'oseille
CREAM OF CAULIFLOWER AND SORREL SOUP 30
Crème de courgettes et d'aubergines au safran
CREAM OF COURGETTES AND AUBERGINES
WITH SAFFRON SOUP 31
Crème de laitue aux pommes fruits
CREAM OF LETTUCE WITH APPLE SOUP 32
Crème de poivrons rouges au gingembre
CREAM OF RED PEPPER WITH GINGER SOUP 33
Potage de petits pois à la menthe
PEAS AND MINT SOUP 34
Soupe au pistou PESTO SOUP 36
Soupe de tomates au basilic
TOMATO AND BASIL SOUP 38
Gaspacho 39
Soupe parmentière 40
Velouté d'asperges aux huîtres
CREAM OF ASPARAGUS WITH OYSTER SOUP 41
Velouté de topinambours au curry
CREAM OF JERUSALEM ARTICHOKE
WITH CURRY SOUP 42
Velouté de pistaches au poivre de Séchuan
CREAM OF PISTACHIO NUT
WITH SICHUAN PEPPER SOUP 43

### SALADS Salades

Salade Baumanière 46
Salade de concombre à l'aneth
CUCUMBER AND DRILL SALAD 47
Salade d'artichauts et fenouil
ARTICHOKES AND FENNEL SALAD 48

Salade d'artichauts & haricots blancs
à la coriandre ARTICHOKE AND WHITE BEAN
WITH CORIANDER SALAD 49
Salade d'endives aux huîtres
CHICORY AND OYSTERS SALAD 50
Salade de cèpes crus au cresson
RAW CEPS AND CRESS SALAD 51
Salade de haricots verts et beignets de morue
GREEN BEANS AND COD FRITTER SALAD 52
Salade de pamplemousse et fenouil
à la badiane GRAPEFRUIT, FENNEL
AND STAR ANISE SALAD 53
Salade de pommes de terre au vandouvan
POTATO SALAD WITH VANDOUVAN 54
Salade de pois gourmands et de ris de veau
SUGAR PEA AND SWEETBREAD SALAD 55
Salade gourmande de truffes
aux pommes de terre
TRUFFLE AND POTATO SALAD 56

### VEGETABLE MAIN DISHES
PLATS DE LÉGUMES

Asperges rôties, jus crémeux aux asperges
ROASTED ASPARAGUS,
WITH CREAMY JUICE/GRAVY 59
Asperges vertes aux dés de foie de canard
GREEN ASPARAGUS WITH DICE
OF DUCK LIVER 60

# Soups,

## SOUPES, POTAGES ET VELOUTÉS

# Crème de chou-fleur à l'oseille

## CREAM OF CAULIFLOWER AND SORREL SOUP

*For 4 :*

a cauliflower,
a small leek,
4 dl of cream,
200 g of sorrel,
salt and pepper,
a glass of vinegar,
20 g of butter,
1 l of chicken stock.

Trim the cauliflower, and soak the curd for a few minutes in water slightly seasoned with vinegar, and strain. Thinly slice the leek, and melt the butter in a pan.

Add in the leek and sweat it slowly. Now, pour in the stock, and season with salt and pepper. When it comes to a boil, you can add the cauliflower. Cover and cook for some time.

Clean the sorrel, rinse it and cook it briefly in a pan without adding water until it sweats.

Put to one side. When the cauliflower is cooked, put it through the blender or the food mill, and then through a small strainer. Pour it in a pan with the sorrel and some cream.

Check the seasoning and make sure the soup is creamy.

# Crème de courgettes et d'aubergines au safran

## CREAM OF COURGETTES AND AUBERGINES WITH SAFFRON SOUP

*For 5 or 6 :*

1 kg of courgettes/zu-
    chinis,
1 kg of aubergines/egg-
    plants,
1 pepper,
a tablespoon of sugar,
1 l of cream,
1 gram of saffron,
Salt and pepper.

START by dicing the courgettes, the pepper, and the aubergines. Heat them in a frying pan with a little olive oil. Season with a little sugar, and some salt and pepper.

When the dice are slightly browned, add in the cream and saffron, and leave to reduce.

Put the courgette and cream through the blender, and then through a small strainer.

You can serve this soup either warm or chilled, but it has to be served very creamy.

# *Crème de laitue aux pommes fruits*

## CREAM OF LETTUCE WITH APPLE SOUP

*For 6 :*

2 kg of lettuce leaves
   without the hearts,
1 l of poultry broth,
3 fruits of star anise,
2 apples.

**B**LANCH the green leaves of the lettuce for a short time in boiling water, refresh them in ice-cold water, drain, and sweat in a little butter. Add in the chicken stock, and then the star anise. Leave to cook for 10 minutes, and pass through the blender.

Sculpt out pearls into the apples and sweat them in fresh butter. Lay them in a dish and pour in the creamy soup.

# *Crème de poivrons rouges au gingembre*

## CREAM OF RED PEPPER WITH GINGER SOUP

200 g of red peppers,
40 g of butter,
25 cl of cream,
10 g of ginger,
25 cl of chicken stock.

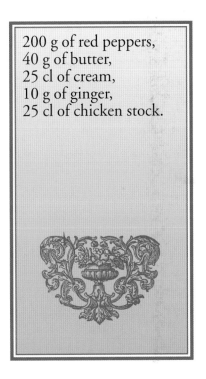

**C**UT the peppers in two lengthways. Seed and roughly dice them. Brown them in a tall pan. When they colour a little, add in the stock and the cream. Leave to cook for 10 minutes.

Pass the soup through the blender. Sprinkle with 10 g of ginger, leave to reduce for 5 minutes and pass through a small strainer.

You can serve this cream as a soup, or as a side dish for fish or crustaceans. It is delicious.

# Potage de petits pois à la menthe

## PEAS AND MINT SOUP

2 kg of fresh garden
  peas,
500 g of potatoes,
50 g of butter,
3 leeks,
1 onion,
fresh mint sprigs .

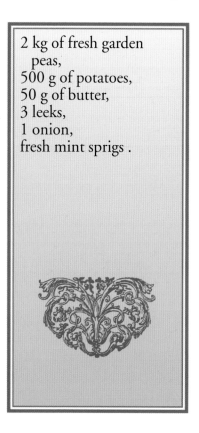

SHELL the garden peas, peel and mince the onion. Peel the potatoes, clean the leeks and roughly cut them up.

In a saucepan, heat on a slow fire 50 g of butter, the minced onion, the leeks, and the mint blades. Cover and cook for 5 minutes. It should sweat, not brown.

Pour in 2 litres of cold water, and turn up the heat. When it comes to a boil, add the potatoes, season with salt and pepper, and simmer for 15 to 20 minutes. When the potatoes are cooked, add the peas and the mint leaves and leave to simmer for 7 more minutes.

Pass the soup through the blender, and refrigerate quickly as the soup would change colour otherwise.

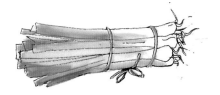

# *Soupe au pistou*

## PESTO SOUP

**For 4 to 6 :**

2 middle-sized leeks,
  only their white
  and light green parts,
  thinly sliced,
175 g of thinly sliced
  onions,
175 g of carrots (cut in
  4, lengthways,
  and thinly minced),
350 g of potatoes (cut in
  4, lengthways,
  and thinly minced),
500 g of fresh white
  beans, shelled,
a bouquet garni with
  a stick of celery,
2.5 l of boiling water,
175 g of fresh
  green beans, cut up,
2 or 3 small firm

Cook the leeks, onions, carrots, potatoes, haricot beans and the bouquet garni in salted boiling water.

Cover and simmer for 30 minutes.

It might be necessary to cook the haricot beans for a little longer, as they need to be very well cooked.

Add the green beans, courgettes and macaronis, and cook for about 15 minutes. (Cooking time will depend on the kind of macaronis and beans you use.)

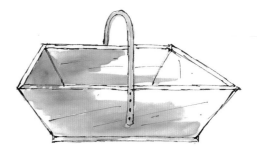

courgettes, sliced.
90 g of short macaroni,
salt,

*For the Pistou :*

4 garlic cloves,
60 g of basil leaves
  and flowers,
Salt and pepper
  from the mill,
90 g of freshly grated
  Parmesan cheese,
1 middle-sized tomato
  peeled and de-seeded,
50 cl of olive oil.

Meanwhile, prepare the pistou. You can use a mortar (the kind used for aïoli in Provence is fine), or a wooden bowl.

# *Soupe de tomates au basilic*

## TOMATO AND BASIL SOUP

1 kg of tomatoes,
4 onions,
3 basil bunches,
Some olive oil,
Salt and pepper,
1/2 l of stock,
1 tomato to garnish
the soup.

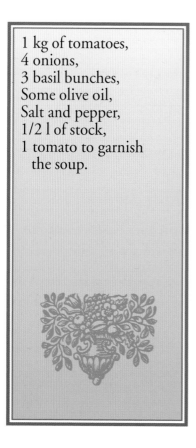

**P**EEL, mince, and sweat the onions. They should be translucent and not browned when you add the peeled and seeded tomatoes.

Gently fry, bring to a boil, and add the roughly chopped potato. Season with salt and pepper and leave to simmer over a gentle heat.

When the soup is cooked, add in the basil leaves, pass through the blender, and then through a small strainer.

Dice a peeled and seeded tomato, and sprinkle over the soup.

# Gaspacho

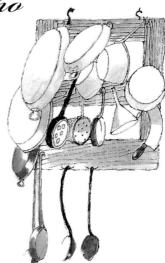

1 kg of tomatoes,
1 cucumber,
1 clove of garlic,
1 tablespoon of ketchup,
1 drop of tabasco sauce,
3 or 4 mint leaves.

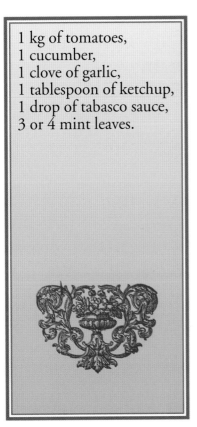

**W**ITH the help of a sharp knife, remove the stalks and the toughest part of the flesh from the tomatoes.

Quickly poach the tomatoes in boiling water and cool them in chilled water to stop the cooking process. The skins should now come off easily.

Pass all the ingredients through the blender, and add a tablespoon of mayonnaise.

Serve chilled.

# Soupe parmentière

1 leek,
1 shallot,
200 g of potatoes,
50 g of butter,
salt,
1 l of chicken
   or vegetable stock,
20 cl of cream.

CLEAN the leek and keep only 50 g taken in its middle. Mince finely. Cook the potatoes in salted water, then peel them and pass 150 g through the blender.

Peel and mince the shallots and sweat them in 50 g of butter in a saucepan. Mince the leeks, water with stock and simmer for four to five minutes. Slowly beat in 150 g of potato purée and 20 cl of cream.

If the soup is too thick, add some stock, remove from the heat, and check the seasoning.

# Velouté d'asperges aux huîtres

## CREAM OF ASPARAGUS WITH OYSTER SOUP

**For 4 :**

1 dozen oysters,
a bunch of green asparagus (about ⌀ 1cm),
3/4 l of cream,
1/4 l of fish stock.

Clean and peel the asparagus, cut the tips off. Cook the tips in salted boiling water, and stop the cooking process by throwing them in chilled water.

Chop the spears, and brown them with butter in a saucepan. Add in the fish stock and the cream and leave to reduce. Pass through the blender, and then through a small strainer.

Open the oysters, slightly warm them, remove them from their shell, lay them in warm plates.

Add the juices in the soup (which can be reduced if necessary), and pour it over the oysters.

Add the asparagus tips, warmed in butter.

# Velouté de topinambours au curry

## CREAM OF JERUSALEM ARTICHOKE WITH CURRY SOUP

500 g of Jerusalem
   artichokes,
1/2 l of chicken stock,
1/4 l of single cream
   or light cream,
a teaspoon of curry,
a teaspoon of honey,
olive oil (preferably from
   the vallée des Baux).

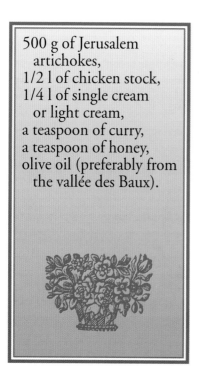

**C**LEAN the Jerusalem artichokes without peeling them. Dice them and brown them in a little olive oil for five minutes in a frying pan.

Add one teaspoon of honey to slightly caramelise the Jerusalem artichokes, then sprinkle them with curry and pour in the chicken stock and the cream.

Simmer for 30 minutes and pass trough a small strainer.

# *Velouté de pistaches au poivre de Séchuan*

## CREAM OF PISTACHIO NUT WITH SICHUAN PEPPER SOUP

*For 6 :*

500 g of pistachio nuts, shelled,
20 g of Sichuan pepper,
10 g of honey,
1/4 l of champagne,
1/4 l of chicken stock,
1/2 l of cream,
the juice of a lemon.

HEAT 10 g of honey in a saucepan over a brisk heat. Once melted, add the whole shelled pistachio nuts, and caramelise them for 5 minutes.

Deglaze with 1/4 l of champagne, and add the chicken stock, and the cream. Pass the soup through the blender, leave to simmer, uncovered, for 45 minutes over a slow heat.

Pass the soup through a small strainer, season with salt and Sichuan pepper and the juice of a lemon before serving.

Add a few chopped pistachio nuts when you serve.

# Salads

## SALADES

# Salade Baumanière

The heart of a lettuce,
2 tomatoes, peeled and
   seeded,
1 slice of raw ham,
100 g of green beans,
50 g of pine nuts,
2 palm hearts,
2 artichokes,
a few basil leaves,
olive oil, preferably from
   the vallée des Baux,
Xeres vinegar.

FIRST, cook the artichokes, seed two tomatoes and slice them. Cook the French beans, which should be kept crisp.

Finely mince the raw ham, and blend all the ingredients together, leaving the pine nuts and the basil leaves on top.

Prepare a French dressing, and blend well. This salad may also be served with 1 dl of whipped cream and a few drops of lemon.

# *Salade de concombres à l'aneth*

## CUCUMBER AND DRILL SALAD

4 cucumbers,
2 garlic cloves,
150 g of yoghurt,
the juice of a lemon,
2 tablespoons of finely
   minced drill,
olive oil, preferably from
   the vallée des Baux,
a few baby spinach
   leaves.

**P**EEL and slice the cucumber first. Lay the slices on a dish, sprinkle them with salt, and leave them for an hour. Mash the garlic so as to obtain purée, and place it in a bowl with yoghurt, the lemon juice, the minced drill, and season with salt and pepper. Clean the spinach leaves.

Blend the cucumber slices with the yoghurt sauce, lay them in the centre of a plate, and sprinkle spinach around the cucumber.

# Salade d'artichauts et fenouil

## ARTICHOKES AND FENNEL SALAD

8 purple artichokes,
the juice of a lemon,
4 fennel bulbs,
1 dl of olive oil,
    preferably from
    the vallée des Baux,
50 g of finely sliced
    Parmesan cheese.

In a hollow dish, pour some water and the juice of a lemon. Remove the artichoke leaves and keep the hearts. Remove the chokes and finely slice the hearts. Place them in lemon juice and water. Slice the fennel as well.

Make a dressing with some olive oil, the juice of a lemon, and season with salt and pepper.

Alternatively place in each plate the fennel and the artichoke, pour dressing on top, and sprinkle with Parmesan.

# *Salade d'artichauts & haricots blancs à la coriandre*

## ARTICHOKE AND WHITE BEAN WITH CORIANDER SALAD

*For 4 :*

12 purple artichokes,
200 g of fresh
    white beans,
0.5 l of white stock,
0.5 l of white wine,
20 g of coriander,
100 g of lardoons (thick
    rashers of streaky
    bacon, diced),
some olive oil,
the juice of a lemon,
salt and pepper,
a bunch of fresh
    coriander.

**R**EMOVE the leaves and the chokes from the artichokes, shell the beans, dice the streaky bacon, and blanch it. Take two saucepans and brown in each of them half the lardoons and the coriander.

Sweat the artichokes in one of them, and the beans in the other. Water both of them with white stock and white wine. Cover and leave to simmer.

For the dressing, take a little cooking juice, some olive oil, the juice of a lemon, and season with salt and pepper.

Leave the beans and the artichokes to cool. Remove the chokes.

Lay the beans and three artichokes in each guest's plate, and sprinkle with fresh coriander. Top with a dash of dressing, and serve chilled.

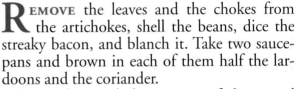

# Salade d'endives aux huîtres

## CHICORY AND OYSTERS SALAD

3 heads of chicory,
1/2 head of celeriac,
16 large oysters,
some peanut oil,
some Xeres vinegar,
a slice of ox tongue
or ham if you prefer.

For each guest, keep four whole chicory leaves, which will be used to place the oysters. Slice the chicory, peel the celeriac and shred half of it into a julienne. Chop the tongue into small sticks.

For the dressing, take 1/4 of vinegar for 3/4 of peanut oil, and add the oyster juice. Season with salt and pepper if necessary.

Mix the sliced chicory, the tongue, the shredded celeriac and the dressing.

In each plate, lay some chicory and celeriac salad, top with four chicory leaves in each of which you will place an oyster.

Sprinkle the oysters with a drop of dressing for service.

# *Salade de cèpes crus*

## *au cresson*

### RAW CEPS AND CRESS SALAD

8 ceps (about 8 cm
  in diameter),
olive oil,
the juice of a lemon,
a bunch of cress,
one spring onion.

WIPE the caps of the mushrooms with a wet cloth. Remove the caps from the stalks, which will be cleaned, and finely minced. Mince the spring onion, and mix it with the stalks .

Finely slice the caps and lay the slices in the plate around the minced stalks and spring onions.

Clean the cress and pass it through the blender to obtain juice. For the dressing, add it to a little olive oil and the juice of a lemon. Sprinkle the dressing around the salad.

# Salade de haricots verts et beignets de morue

## GREEN BEANS AND COD FRITTER SALAD

*For 4 :*

400 g of green beans,
800 g of cod,
3 tablespoons
   of cod brandade,
33 cl of beer,
150 g of flour,
25 g of yeast,
olive oil,
Xeres vinegar,
mustard,
peanut oil.

CLEAN the green beans, and cook them for 5 minutes in salted water, uncovered, and drain. Cool them with water and ice cubes and drain again.

For the dressing, add 1 tablespoon of Xeres vinegar, some salt and pepper, and 3 tablespoons of olive oil to 1 tablespoon of mustard.

Flatten the fillets so that they are 5 mm thick, and season them with olive oil and lemon juice. Stuff them with cod brandade (blended cod, garlic and olive oil) and roll them to form "sausages". Cut 3 slices of cod for each guest.

Prepare the batter : mix the flour, the yeast and the beer together, and whip.

Heat the peanut oil. It should reach 200 °C (400°F). Dip the cod slices in the batter and deep fry them.

Sprinkle the green beans with dressing and lay the salad and the fritters around.

# Salade de pamplemousse et fenouil à la badiane

## GRAPEFRUIT, FENNEL AND STAR ANISE SALAD

2 grapefruits,
2 heads of fennel,
1/4 l of water,
125 g of sugar,
4 fruits of star anise.

**M**AKE a syrup with water, sugar and star anise. Bring it to a boil and leave to infuse. Clean the fennel heads and mince them. Poach one in the syrup, and keep the other one raw.

Peel the grapefruits and cut them into supremes. Keep the juice.

In a soup plate lay the grapefruit supremes, the raw and poached shredded fennel and top with syrup and grapefruit juice.

# Salade de pommes de terre au vandouvan

## POTATO SALAD WITH VANDOUVAN

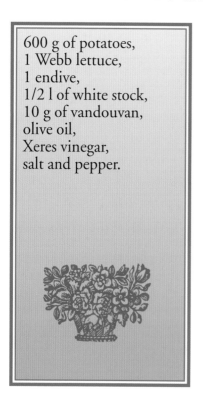

600 g of potatoes,
1 Webb lettuce,
1 endive,
1/2 l of white stock,
10 g of vandouvan,
olive oil,
Xeres vinegar,
salt and pepper.

PEEL and slice the potatoes, and set them in a saucepan. Water with the white stock and the vandouvan. Bring to a boil, and simmer slowly. Remove the stock, and lay the potatoes aside.

Make a dressing with a little olive oil, some Xeres vinegar, some salt and pepper, and a dash of the potatoes cooking juice.

Clean the salads, and lay the salad in the centre of a plate, the potato slices around it, and sprinkle with dressing.

# Salade de pois gourmands et de ris de veau

## SUGAR PEA AND SWEETBREAD SALAD

**For 4 :**

600 g of calf sweetbread,
1 kg of sugar peas,
2 dl of chicken stock,
1 egg,
50 g of flour,
100 g of walnuts,
mustard,
olive oil,
vinegar.

SOAK the sweetbread in cold water for about 12 hours. Blanch and trim it to remove any unwanted part. Braise it quickly in chicken stock until it is not quite cooked yet.

Chop it into 2 square centimetres dice. Beat the egg in a little water, and drop the sweetbread dice in flour first, then in the beaten egg, and in grounded walnuts at last.

Cook the peas in salted boiling water, uncovered, for 3 minutes and cool them quickly in chilled water.

Make a dressing with mustard, 1 tablespoon of vinegar for 3 of olive oil, and sprinkle it on the peas. Set them on a plate.

Deep fry the sweetbread dice in peanut oil, and lay them around the peas.

# Salade gourmande de truffes aux pommes de terre

## TRUFFLE AND POTATO SALAD

80 g of truffles,
200 g of lamb's lettuce,
4 large potatoes,
Xeres vinegar,
olive oil,
the juice of a lemon,
salt and pepper.

**FINELY** slice the truffles. Make a dressing with 1 tablespoon of Xeres vinegar, 3 tablespoons of olive oil, and the juice of a lemon.

Clean the lamb's lettuce carefully, and dry it. Mix it in a salad bowl with half of the dressing.

Peel the potatoes and cut them into pieces the size of truffles with a punch. Then slice them finely. Sauté them in olive oil and butter in a frying pan.

On each plate, lay some lamb's lettuce, topped with slices of raw truffles and warm potatoes.

# Vegetable

## main dishes

### PLATS DE LÉGUMES

# *Asperges rôties, jus crémeux aux asperges*

## ROASTED ASPARAGUS, WITH CREAMY JUICE/GRAVY

*For 2 :*

12 middle size
  spears/ asparagus,
20 g of butter,
10 g of Parmesan cheese,
10 cl of poultry extract,
2.5 dl of whipped
  cream,
salt and pepper,
barberry fruits,
the juice of an orange.

**C**LEAN the spears asparagus, and leave 10 cm only. Cook the tips in boiling water for 10 minutes. Roughly cut up the stalks and cook them for a quarter of an hour in the poultry extract. Press the stalks through a sieve and reduce.

Brown the asparagus tips with a little butter in a frying pan and sprinkle with grated cheese.

Cook the fruits in the orange juice for 2 minutes.

Set the asparagus in a plate and add the asparagus juice mixed with whipped cream and barberry fruits, which can be replaced by poppy petals, blanched for 2 minutes in a mixture of water and honey over a slow fire.

# *Asperges vertes aux dés de foie de canard*

## GREEN ASPARAGUS WITH DICE OF DUCK LIVER

*For 4 :*

1.5 kg of green
   asparagus,
200 g of duck liver,
20 g of butter,
1 tablespoon of vinegar,
10 cl of olive oil,
2 eggs.

Cook the asparagus in boiling and salted water. Dice the livers, in order to obtain 1 centimetre cubes. Cook the eggs for about ten minutes, shell them, and dice the white and the yolk separately.

Quickly brown the asparagus tips in a little butter, and fry the liver for 1 minute on each side.

Remove the fat from the frying pan, deglaze the latter with vinegar, and whip the gravy with olive oil. Sprinkle the asparagus with the foie gras and add the dressing.

Finally, sprinkle the dish with the egg dice.

# Gâteau d'asperges

## ASPARAGUS CAKE

1 kg of asparagus,
2 whole eggs,
1 egg yolk,
a hint of grated nutmeg,
4 tablespoons of fresh
tomato coulis.

**P**EEL the asparagus, rinse them and cook them in salted boiling water for 10 minutes. Strain, and put 12 tips to one side.

Pass the asparagus through the blender, and then through a small strainer to remove the scales or tough parts. Pour the purée in a saucepan, and reduce over a slow fire.

Mix the asparagus purée with the whole eggs and the egg yolk, and add the ground nutmeg. Season with salt and pepper.

Grease some ramekins with butter, and fill them with purée. Cook au bain-marie in a 200° (400°F) hot oven. Brown the asparagus tips in butter and set them around the asparagus flans, turned out over a plate.

Top with a tomato coulis (cf. p.106)
Follow the same instructions for spinach or carrot flans.

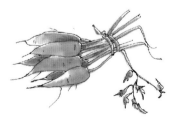

# Assiette aux trois poireaux

## THREE LEEKS PLATE

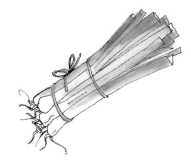

3 leeks,
1 dl of cream,
10 g of butter,
1 l of olive or peanut oil,
a little gravy,
salt and pepper.

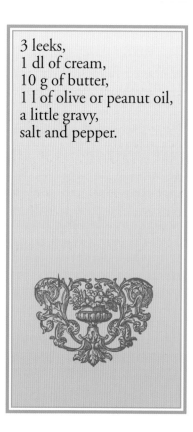

CLEAN the leeks and remove the green parts. Slice one leek into a fine julienne (thin strips) and fry it in peanut oil.

Finely dice the second leek, and sweat it with 1 dl of cream until it forms a compote.

Slice the third leek sideways and sauté it in butter.

Set the compote in the centre of the plate, then the sautéed leek and finally the fried julienne on top.

Add a dash of gravy around it when you serve.

# *Terrine d'artichauts à la crème de ciboulette*

## ARTICHOKES TERRINE WITH CHIVES CREAM

4 kg of artichokes,
1 l of cream,
8 egg yolks,
salt and pepper,
chives,
1 tablespoon of flour.

**R**EMOVE the leaves from the artichokes to keep only the hearts. Blanch them in a mixture of water and flour, remove the chokes and slice the hearts.

Set the artichokes in a terrine, sprinkling minced chives over each layer.

Blend the cream and the egg yolks, and pour it over the artichokes.

Cook in the oven, au bain-marie, for 30 minutes, then leave to cool for 12 hours. Turn out the terrine and slice it.

Serve with a sauce made of whipped cream and chives.

# Mousseline d'artichauts

## ARTICHOKE MOUSSELINE

16 small artichokes,
1/2 l of cream,
the juice of a lemon,
1 tablespoon of flour,
5 cl of truffle juice,
10 g of butter.

TAKE some small artichokes, remove their leaves, and cook the hearts in salted water, with the juice of a lemon and a tablespoon of flour. It should prevent the hearts from darkening.

Cook them until they are soft, and pass them through a small strainer.

Stir this purée, either with a whip or a wooden spoon, and add in the saucepan 1/2 l of cream, 2 knobs of butter, and 5 cl of truffle juice.

Season with salt and pepper from the mill if necessary. This mousseline should be soft and light.

# Artichauts à la barigoule

12 small purple
   artichokes,
100 g of Parma ham,
100 g of streaky bacon,
2 mushrooms,
1 shallot,
1 twig of parsley,
2 tablespoons of olive
oil,
1 tablespoon of gravy,
1 dl of chicken stock.

Cut the top of the artichokes leaves off, and remove the external leaves. Remove the chokes and stuff the artichokes with finely minced bacon, ham, mushrooms, shallot, and parsley, mixed with a little olive oil and butter.

Tie the artichokes with string to prevent the stuffing from falling when the artichokes are being cooked.

Set the artichokes in a saucepan lined with bacon and top them with more bacon. Water with gravy and stock and cover with foil or greaseproof paper. Cook over a brisk heat for 45 minutes.

When the artichokes are cooked, remove the strings, add a dash of cream to the sauce and leave to reduce, add a little lemon juice before serving.

# Fèves nouvelles à la menthe fraîche

## FRESH BROAD BEANS AND MINT

2 kg of shelled
  broad beans,
20 cl of cream,
2 tablespoons
  of chopped mint,
salt and pepper.

CHOOSE fresh broad beans rather than dried ones if you can, even if that means more work to shell them. They are tender, and less floury, and taste delicious.

Cook the broad beans for 3 to 4 minutes according to their size, reduce the cream in a frying pan, and throw in the strained beans.

Sprinkle with minced mint, season with salt and pepper, and stir carefully, to prevent the beans crushing.

pepsil

# Indienne d'aubergines

500 g of
   aubergines/eggplants,
50 g of fresh ginger,
4 garlic cloves,
2 bay leaves,
2 tablespoons of sherry,
30 cl of sesame oil,
salt and pepper,
2 tablespoons of honey,
2 tablespoons
   of mustard seeds,
1 tablespoon of cumin.

CLEAN the aubergines, and dice them. Fry the dice in sesame oil, and drain off the oil. Add 2 tablespoons of honey, 50 g of finely minced ginger, 2 tablespoons of sherry and 1 of cumin. Cook over a slow heat for 15 to 20 minutes.

Before serving, add 2 tablespoons of mustard seeds.

Indienne d'aubergines can be served as a side dish for pasta or fish.

# Caviar d'aubergines

## AUBERGINES CAVIAR

**For 6 :**

6 medium-sized
    aubergines/eggplants,
1 large onion,
olive oil,
salt and pepper,
black olives,
chopped parsley.

**P**UT the aubergines on to a grill over embers, or wrapped in foil in a hot oven. Turn them over frequently, until they are quite soft. Holding the stalk, peel them, and leave them to drain for half an hour.

Mash the pulp, mince the onion, and mix it with the aubergine purée, then slowly add olive oil, and whip up as for a mayonnaise.

Season with salt and pepper.

Add a little minced parsley and some sliced black olives.

This dish may be served warm, or chilled.

# Aubergines en caton

4 medium-sized
   aubergines/eggplants,
a bunch of basil,
2 garlic cloves,
olive oil.

**P**RICK the aubergines with a fork. Place them on a baking tray in a hot oven (200°C, 400°F) for 25 minutes. Skin the garlic cloves, mince them finely with basil, and pound this mixture, in a bowl, with four tablespoons of olive oil. Season with salt and pepper. Blend well with a fork.

Remove the aubergines from the oven, cut them in two, and top the halves with the mixture of garlic, basil and olive oil.

The aubergines en caton should be eaten with spoons.

# Mille-feuille d'aubergines à la cardamome

## AUBERGINE AND CARDAMOM MILLE-FEUILLE

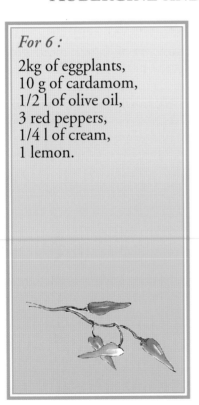

**For 6 :**

2kg of eggplants,
10 g of cardamom,
1/2 l of olive oil,
3 red peppers,
1/4 l of cream,
1 lemon.

MAKE a caviar d'aubergines. Remove the stalks, and wrap them in foil. Bake them for half an hour in a preheated oven.

Then, cut the aubergines in two, and with the help of a spoon, remove the pulp, which should come off easily if thoroughly cooked. Add a dash of olive oil to this purée, as well as a little cardamom. Put to one side.

Slice the aubergines very finely, flour the slices, and fry them in olive oil until they are crisp.

Dice the red peppers, and sauté them in olive oil in a saucepan. When their colour changes to a lighter shade, add some cream, and leave to simmer very slowly. Pass through a small strainer.

On each plate, lay some caviar d'aubergines, topped with aubergine fritters, then some more caviar, fritters, etc, so as to form a mille feuilles. Finally, sprinkle pepper cream around the mille-feuille.

# Gratin d'aubergines

4 aubergines/eggplants,
20 cl of olive oil,
basil,
breadcrumbs.

*For the concassée
de tomates :*

2 kg of tomatoes,
1 onion,
3 garlic cloves,
4 tablespoons
   of olive oil,
1 tablespoon
   of caster sugar,
1 tablespoon
   of tomato concentré,
basil or tarragon,
3 twigs of parsley,
a twig of thyme,
1 bay leaf.

BOTH the tomato mixture and the aubergines can be prepared beforehand, but the gratin needs to be served immediately after baking. Preheat the oven, with a dish containing a little water, for the bain-marie. To prevent the water from boiling, lay a folded newspaper sheet at the bottom of the bain-marie dish.

*For the concassée de tomates :*

Skin the garlic. Peel and mince the onion. Remove their stalks, and blanch the tomatoes to remove their skin. Cool them in chilled water to stop the cooking process. Chop the tomatoes, and remove the seeds and the pulp. In a stewpot, eat the whole garlic cloves in olive oil. Add the minced onion, and sweat it slightly, as it should not brown. Add the tomato flesh, the tomato concentré, and season with salt and pepper, caster sugar, parsley, thyme, bay leaf, and eventually a few leaves of tarragon or basil. Leave to simmer for an hour on a slow fire.

### *The gratin :*

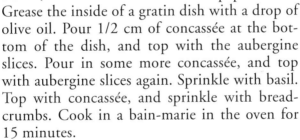

Peel the aubergines, and slice them lengthways into 3 mm thick slices. Heat 20 cl of olive in a frying pan, and fry the aubergines slices on both sides until they change colour. Fry a few at a time, and drain them on kitchen paper.

Grease the inside of a gratin dish with a drop of olive oil. Pour 1/2 cm of concassée at the bottom of the dish, and top with the aubergine slices. Pour in some more concassée, and top with aubergine slices again. Sprinkle with basil. Top with concassée, and sprinkle with breadcrumbs. Cook in a bain-marie in the oven for 15 minutes.

# Cardons à la moelle

## CARDOONS AND MARROW

1 cardoon head
  (you need 750 g),
20 cl of cream,
1 tablespoon of flour,
a knob of butter,
some Gruyère
  or swiss cheese,
60 g of marrow.

CLEAN the cardoons. Remove the tough ribs, and the leaves. Scrape the ribs, and strip off the fibres and prickles on the outside.

Cut the ribs into 10 cm sections, and brush them with lemon juice.

Take some water, and add a tablespoon of flour diluted in lemon juice. Bring to a boil, drop in the cardoons, cover, and simmer for 2 hours.

Reduce 20 cl of cream, brown the cardoons with a knob of butter, and mix them with the cream. Lay them in a gratin dish.

Poach the beef marrow in salted water, drain it, and slice it roughly.

Top the cardoons with marrow, sprinkle with grated cheese, and cook au bain-marie in the oven for 20 minutes.

# Chou à l'estragon

## KALE AND TARRAGON

*For 4 :*

25 leaves of kale,
6 rashers of smoked
   streaky bacon,
2 spring onions,
50 g of butter,
1 bunch of tarragon,
some salt and pepper.

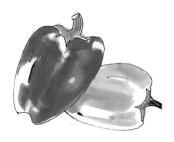

Take the nicest kale leaves you can get. Remove the central ribs, and blanch them in salted boiling water.

Chop the bacon rashers, and mince finely the onions, and the tarragon leaves.

Roughly chop the kale leaves. In a saucepan, heat 50 g of butter and the bacon and onion.

When the butter starts to foam, add the cabbage and season with salt and pepper.

Leave to simmer slowly for 10 minutes, or enough time for the cabbage to warm.

Add in the minced tarragon, mix, and serve warm.

# Endives à l'orange

## ORANGE AND CHICORY

400 g of chicory,
1 orange,
20 g of butter,
1/2 lemon,
20 g of caster sugar,
oil,
salt and pepper.

Take a piece of the peel of an orange, and chop it in a very thin julienne. Express the orange juice.

Chop the chicory sideways. Put them with 20 g of caster sugar, some salt and pepper, 4 tablespoons of orange juice and a knob of butter, and heat over a brisk heat for a few minutes, and then over a slower heat until the orange juice evaporates.

Blanch the orange peel to remove its bitterness, and blend it with the chicory.

You might serve this dish with pasta or scallops for example.

# Petits navets confits

## CONFITS TURNIPS

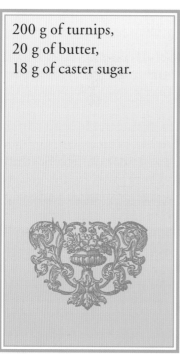

200 g of turnips,
20 g of butter,
18 g of caster sugar.

**P**EEL the turnips. You might eventually flute them, that is carve them with a special knife from top to bottom, so as to obtain fluted slices. Slice the turnips 3 to 4 mm thick.

Bring water to a boil, and throw the turnips in the saucepan. Leave them to cook for 4 minutes, then cool them in chilled water to stop the cooking process, and then drain them.

Melt 15 g of butter in a frying pan, and add 2 tablespoons of water, and 1 tablespoon of caster sugar. Simmer the turnip slices very slowly.
They should not brown, and they are cooked when the cooking juice starts to caramelise.

They must be firm, but not crisp. If they need to be cooked a little longer, add a tablespoon of water before putting the saucepan back on the fire.

Once cooked, they should be kept warm.
This dish might be served with poelé duck liver escalopes.

# Fenouil au four

## BAKED FENNEL

*For 4 :*

1 kg of baby fennel,
1/2 bunch of coriander,
2 seeds of star anise,
1 l of white wine,
olive oil,
salt and pepper,
100 g of streaky bacon.

HEAT the olive oil in a saucepan, and add the cleaned baby fennel, brown them slightly, and deglaze with white wine, coriander and star anise as well as some salt and pepper and chopped bacon.

Bake the fennel in a 220°C hot oven for 30 to 40 minutes.

Remove the fennel and drain. Reduce the cooking juice and pass it through a small strainer.

# Fleurs de courgettes farcies à ma façon

## COURGETTES FLOWERS STUFFED MY WAY

*For 4 :*

50 g of croutons,
10 g of single leaved
   parsley,
20 g of roasted pine nuts,
a hint of minced garlic,
20 g Parmesan cheese,
   cut into thin strips,
10 g of stoned black olives,
50 g of fried diced
   aubergine,
16 courgettes/zucchinis,
   and their flowers.

*For the batter,*
*you will need :*

110 g of flour,
33 cl of beer,
40 g of yeast.

*Mix all the ingredients and*
*use immediately if possible.*

Put 4 flowers to one side. Cut the flowers off from the courgettes, and open them. Chop 150 g of the courgettes sideways. Remove the pistils from the flowers.

Blanch the chopped courgettes for 3 minutes, hold the 12 flowers above the boiling water, and blanch them as well for 1 minute. Drain them on kitchen paper.

Prepare the stuffing with the rest of the ingredients, mix , and stuff the 12 flowers. Make the batter.

Lay the 4 flowers on a baking tray, and brush them with batter. Deep fry them in peanut oil (make sure the oil is not too hot), only on the batter side. The flowers should not brown. Set them on the baking tray, and dry them for 24 hours in a 60° hot oven.

Make a dressing with olive oil, and balsamic vinegar. Slightly warm up the stuffed flowers in the oven. Lay them on a plate, one fried flower in its centre, and sprinkle each stuffed flower with dressing.

# Gratin de courgettes

## COURGETTE AU GRATIN

1 kg of
    courgettes/zucchinis,
1 l of cream,
olive oil,
salt and pepper,
60 g of Parmesan cheese,
150 g of cultivated
    mushrooms,
30 g of butter,
chives.

**P**EEL the courgettes with a paring knife, slice them into 3 mm thick slices, and braise them in olive oil until they are quite soft. Season with salt and pepper, and drain.

Slice the cultivated mushrooms and braise them in butter. Season with salt and pepper.

Pour the cream in a saucepan, and reduce it until it becomes slightly thicker.

Set the courgettes and the mushrooms in a gratin dish, pour in the cream and the minced chives, and sprinkle with grated cheese.

Cook au gratin in the oven.

# Gratin de cèpes farcis

## STUFFED CEPS AU GRATIN

12 fine ceps,
2 chicken livers,
50 g of streaky bacon,
1 shallot,
a few tarragon leaves,
1 egg yolk,
75 g of grated
  Parmesan cheese,
100 g of butter,
olive oil,
100 g of veal
  mincemeat,
some white part
  of a bread, soaked
  in milk.

WIPE the ceps with a wet cloth. Clean the mushrooms, and remove the caps from the stalks. Set the caps in a large frying pan, and sweat them slowly for some time. Then, place them upside down –the hollow side up– in a preheated oven for 5 minutes. Drain and leave to cool down.

Meanwhile, mince the good part of the stalks, the bacon, the chicken livers, the shallot and the tarragon leaves. Mix with the veal mincemeat.

Quickly brown this stuffing in a little olive oil, and some white part of a bread soaked in milk to hold the stuffing ingredients together. Remove the pan from the heat, and add an egg yolk, and a hint of curry.

Brush the mushroom caps with olive oil, and season them with salt and pepper. Stuff all the caps, and lay them in a gratin dish. Sprinkle them with grated Parmesan cheese, top with melted butter, and bake gently in a preheated oven for 15 minutes.

# Croustade de cèpes

*For the puff pastry, you will need :*

250 g of flour,
150 g of butter,
80 cl of cold butter,
7 g of salt,
70 g of melted butter,
800 g of fresh ceps,
olive oil,
salt and pepper,
25 g of shallot,
250 g of cream,
1 egg.

I N a hollow dish, pour 10 cl of water and 7 g of salt. Add 35 g of melted butter, and 200 g of flour. Quickly knead the pastry, gather it into a ball, and draw a deep cross on it with a sharp knife. Lay it on clingfilm and refrigerate it for half an hour.

Then, take 150g of butter out of the fridge, set it on greaseproof paper, and roll it out with a rolling spin into a 10 cm square, 1 cm thick.

The butter should not be too firm. Flour it slightly, and take the pastry out of the fridge.

Roll it out first to form a circle, and then a cross. Place the butter in the cross, and fold the 4 sides so as to wrap the butter.

Slightly flour, and roll the square again into a (30 cm x10 cm) rectangle. Fold it in three to obtain a 10 cm square. Give the pastry a quarter turn on the left, flour it, roll it out again in a (30 cm x 10 cm) rectangle, and fold it in three again. Push two fingers in the pastry as a sign that the first part of the process is over, and refrigerate it for half an hour.

Follow the same instructions again, push four fingers in the pastry this time, and refri-

gerate it for another 30 minutes. Then do the same again for the last time, stuck 6 fingers in the pastry, and refrigerate for half an hour.

Meanwhile, wipe the ceps with a wet cloth. Dice and sauté them, add the minced shallot and the cream. Reduce, season, and put to one side.

Take the pastry and roll it out again. Punch 2 circles, (8 cm diameter) for each guest, one on the top of the other, brush some egg yolk over them, one of them with a hole in its middle.

Lay them on a baking tray, one on top of the other, brush some egg yolk over them, and bake in a 250°C oven for 8 to 10 minutes.

Remove the pastry from the oven, and leave to cool down. Fill the first circle with the sautéed ceps, and top with the second one.

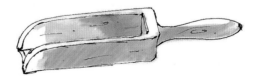

# Raviolis de truffes aux poireaux

## TRUFFLE AND LEEK RAVIOLI

For 6 :

**For 500 g of ravioli pasta :**
400 g of flour,
15 g of salt,
4 whole eggs, 5 yolks.

25 g of fresh truffles,
4 leeks,
300 g of veal sweetbread,
salt and pepper,
a carrot, an onion,
and a stick of celery,
1 dl of cream,
1/8 l of truffle juice,
20 cl of white wine,
100 g of butter.

FOR the pasta, mix 400 g of flour, 15 g of salt, 4 whole eggs, and 5 yolks. Blend well, and allow to rest for 2 hours. Divide it into 2 parts, which should be rolled out very thinly.

Soak the sweetbread in cold water, and trim it, then brown with a chopped carrot, onion, and stick of celery with a knob of butter. Water with white wine, cover, and bake in the oven for 20 minutes.

Remove the sweetbread, leave it to cool down, and trim it again if necessary. Then dice it.

Braise the white parts of the leeks, cut into small squares, in a little water and butter.
Make a sauce with 1/2 l of water and the green part of the leeks. Simmer for half an hour.

Pass it through the blender, then through a small strainer, and add 1 dl of cream and 100 g of butter. Reduce, and add the truffle juice before you serve.

You can choose any form you like for the

raviolis. Brush the rolled out pasta with a brush dipped in a beaten egg.

Set one slice of fresh truffle for each ravioli, as well as one dice of braised sweetbread, and a teaspoon of cooked leek. Season, top with the other part of the pasta, press well around each ravioli, and cut up.

Poach the ravioli in salted water for 5 minutes, strain well, and serve with the warmed sauce.

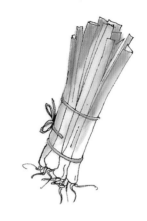

# Mille-feuille de blettes aux truffes

## CHARD AND TRUFFLE MILLE-FEUILLE

*For 6 :*
6 small heads of chard,
90 g of truffles,
1 head of celeriac,
60 cl of truffle juice,
10 cl of single cream,
salt,
2 tablespoons of butter,
chicken stock.

CLEAN the chard, and throw the whole chard in boiling salted water, and add the juice of a lemon. The card shoud be firm.
Strain, and cut them into 10cm x 5cm rectangles. Cook 30 g of fresh truffles in 2 tablespoons of chicken stock, and pass through the blender.

Make a celery purée : peel it and dice it.
Cook it into1/4 l of milk and 3/4 l of salted water. Once cooked, strain them, mash it and add some cream.

On a rectangle of chard leaf, set a layer of minced truffle, a layer of purée, another layer of truffle, and another chard leaf. Bake this mille-feuille in the oven (180 °C, 350°F) for 20 minutes.

In a slightly reduced chicken stock whipped with butter, add the truffle juice. Season with salt and pepper, and whip.

Sprinkle the plate with sauce and set the mille-feuille in its centre. Before serving, add a few thin slices of truffle.

# Fantaisie en blanc & noir

2 black Mélanosporum
   truffles, about
   20 g each,
2 white truffles,
   about 20 g each
   as well,
50 g of butter,
4 slices of
   farmhouse bread,
parsley,
a little armagnac.

SLICE the truffles very thinly. Lay them in a bowl with a dash of armagnac and leave them to marinate. Toast the bread and spread it with soft butter, then set alternatively a slice of white truffle, then a slice of black truffle until the toast is covered. Sprinkle with minced parsley, season with salt and pepper, and serve.

# Mousseline de céleris-raves

## CELERIAC MOUSSELINE

*For 4 :*

2 heads of celeriac,
1/2 l of milk,
40 g of cream cheese,
salt and pepper,
10 cl of cream,
a knob of butter.

PEEL the celeriac, chopped it roughly, throw it in a saucepan, water with milk, season with salt, and simmer. Once cooked, strain and pass through a food mill. Add in the cream and the cream cheese before serving to make the mousseline soft. Warm it in a saucepan and add a knob of butter. Season with salt again if necessary.

A potato may be added to the celeriac to thicken the mousseline.

# Oignons frits

## FRIED ONIONS

2 onions, preferably
  middle-sized,
salt,
100 g of flour,
oil,
20 dl of milk.

PEEL the onions, cut them into 5 mm thick slices. Season with salt, dip them in milk, then flour.

Shake them so that not much flour sticks on them, and fry them in very hot oil.

Strain the onions on kitchen paper, and season with salt again.

Fried onions are served with rib steak or chicken for example.

# Confiture d'oignons

500 g of onions
20 g of butter
20 g of caster sugar
5 cl of Xeres vinegar
5 cl of grenadine syrup
75 cl of red wine
25 cl of dry white wine

ONION jam is delicious served with pâtés. Start by peeling the onions, and mince them finely.

Melt 20 g of butter in a frying pan over a brisk heat, throw in the onions and 20 g of caster sugar and stir continuously until the onions start to caramelise.

Pour 5 cl of grenadine syrup in the pan and stir some more until the grenadine colours the onions.

Add 5 cl of Xeres vinegar, 75 cl of red wine, and 25 cl of white wine. Stir well, and bring to a boil.

Reduce, stirring very frequently so that it does not burn or stick, until the liquid evaporates, and only jam is left.

# Poivrons farcis à la brousse

## RED PEPPERS STUFFED WITH RICOTTA

12 baby peppers,
olive oil,
250 g of ricotta,
1 garlic clove,
30 g of single
   leaved parsley,
salt and pepper,
10 g of minced shallot,
20 g of breadcrumbs,
2 egg yolks.

**B**AKE the peppers in the oven for some time to remove their skin more easily. Cut the top of the peppers to remove the stalks, and marinate them in olive oil. Season with salt and pepper.

For the stuffing, mix the ricotta with a minced garlic clove, 30g of minced parsley, 10 g of minced shallot, the breadcrumbs, and the yolks.

Stuff the drained peppers with it and lay them on a baking tray. Bake them for 30 to 35 minutes.

Set them on a plate with rocket, and a dressing made of walnut oil and balsamic vinegar.

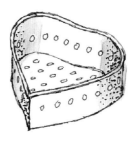

# Petits légumes farcis

## STUFFED VEGETABLES

**For 4 :**

4 small round
  courgettes/zucchinis,
4 onions,
4 small
  aubergines/eggplants,
4 small red peppers,
4 cultivated mushrooms,
2 kg of cultivated
  mushrooms for
  the stuffing.

The pulp of each vegetable will be mixed with minced mushrooms, and stuffed in again. Start by cleaning and mincing the mushrooms, then brown them in butter with a hint of chopped shallot. Stir well to evaporate all the mushrooms juices.

### a. Courgettes :

Cook them in salted water for 5 minutes, remove them from the water, drain them and cut a top in each of them. Mix the pulp with the mushrooms (1/3 mushrooms, 2/3 courgettes), stuff the courgettes, lay them on a greased baking tray, and sprinkle with parmesan cheese, and bake until soft.

### b. Onions :

Do the same with onions. Remove their outer skin, and poach them in water.
Mix the inside of the onion to an equal quantity of mushrooms. Bake them in the oven.

### c. Aubergines and red peppers :

Bake them in the oven at first, instead of poaching them. Remove their pulp, mix it with mushrooms, stuff them, and bake them again.

### d. Mushrooms :

The mushrooms are not cooked before stuffing, but brushed with lemon juice to prevent them from changing colour. The stalks are used for the stuffing. Sprinkle with Parmesan cheese, and bake them in the oven. Cooking times are different for every vegetable, make sure they are not too soft after the first cooking, as they need to hold the stuffing together.

# Pommes de terre écrasées
## au beurre de ciboulette

### MASHED POTATO AND CHIVES BUTTER

400 g of potatoes,
200 g of fresh butter,
2 bunches of chives,
salt and pepper,
olive oil.

MAKE a pommade with the butter and the minced chives, and pass it through a small strainer. Clean the potatoes, and cook them in their jackets in salted water. Once cooked, peel them and crush them with a fork, and add in knobs of chives butter you made earlier.

Season with salt and pepper and pour in a dash of olive oil.

# Pommes de terre soufflées

## SOUFFLÉ POTATOES

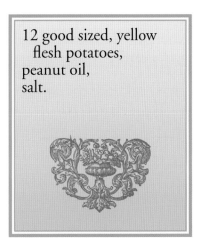

12 good sized, yellow
   flesh potatoes,
peanut oil,
salt.

**P**EEL the potatoes, cut them into slices 3 mm thick, strain the slices in a cloth.
Heat the frying oil, slowly, and throw the slices in little by little. Wait a few minutes and raise the temperature. Stir continuously.
   Remove the potatoes and strain them.
Heat the frying oil as much as possible, and throw the potatoes back in. When they puff and change colour, strain them, season them with salt and serve immediately.

*This recipe is not original, but very few restaurant have it on the menu nowadays.*

# Purée de pommes de terre à l'huile d'olive

*For 4 :*

360 g of peeled pota-
toes,
1.2 dl of cream,
1.2 dl of olive oil,
   preferably from
   Maussane,
salt and pepper,
cayenne pepper.

Cook the peeled potatoes in salted boiling water. When cooked, pass them through the food mill. Slowly heat it with a dash of cream.

Stir with a wooden spoon until the cream is absorbed, add the olive oil, and stir continuously.

When the oil is absorbed as well, season with salt, pepper, and cayenne pepper.

# Ragoût de haricots blancs et chanterelles

## HARICOT BEANS AND CHANTERELLES STEW

*For 4 :*

1 kg of haricot beans,
  for shelling,
1 carrot,
1 onion,
1 clove,
100 g of butter,
300 g of chanterelles,
1 shallot,
chives,
salt and pepper,
a bouquet garni,
1 peeled and seeded
  tomato,
1 spring onion.

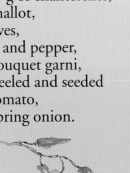

SHELL the haricot beans, clean and strain them. Clean the chanterelles, and peel the carrot, the onion and the shallot.

Throw the beans in a saucepan filled with cold water, and bring to a boil. Throw in the carrot, onion and bouquet garni, and leave to simmer for 40 minutes. Leave to cool down. Sauté the chanterelles and the minced shallot and chives.

Dice the tomato. Sauté the beans with 30 g of butter, throw in the chanterelles, season with salt and pepper add the tomato and the chopped spring onion.

Stir and warm for a few minutes, then serve.

# Gratin dauphinois Baumanière

**For 6 :**

1.5 kg of potatoes,
75 cl of cream,
1 garlic clove.

**P**EEL the potatoes, and cut them into 2 mm thick slices. Ideally, you should use a mandoline for this. Place the potatoes in a bowl, season with salt and pepper and stir well. Rub the inside of a gratin dish with a clove of garlic.

Pour 75 cl of cream in the dish and heat it. No matter what people usually believe, cream does not curdle when heated. Reduce the cream to its half until it is very soft. Using a fork, set the potato slices one at a time in the gratin dish, to coat them with cream, and level the cream. Slowly bring the cream to a boil, and leave to reduce for 5 more minutes

Remove the dish and cook it au bain-marie in the oven. When the gratin changes colour, cover it with foil.

Cooking time will depend on your oven and on what kind of potato you use. In a hot oven, 25 minutes might be enough, but make that 50 in a slower oven. Note that you can make this gratin a little beforehand as it can be kept in a warm oven for an hour or so.

The gratin is cooked when the potatoes feel soft when pricked with a knife.

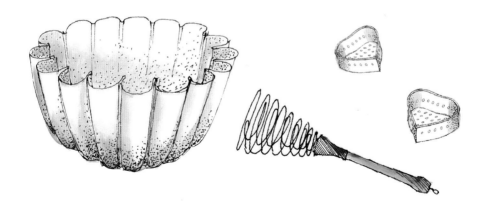

# Ravioles glacées de céleris, aux champignons de saison, à l'orange

## CELERIAC AND MUSHROOM RAVIOLES, ORANGE SAUCE

*For 8 :*

3 celeriac heads,
2 l of fowl stock,
1 kg of mushrooms,
the juice of 6 oranges,
a piece of
   an orange peel,
2 dl of cream,
1 bunch of chives,
3 shallots,
the juice of a lemon.

Cook the celeriac heads with the stock for 20 minutes, and leave it to cool down. When cool, cut the celeriac slices in 2 cm thick slices. Using a bowl, punch them so that they all have the same dimension. Put to one side.

Sweat the minced shallots, as well as the minced mushrooms, add in the orange juice, and add a piece of the orange peel and reduce until the juice evaporates. Leave to cool down.

Stuff the celeriac slices, and wrap them.
Wipe up the cream or yoghurt, and add in the minced chives and the juice of a lime.

# Tarte aux épinards

## SPINACH PIE

A 20 cm rolled out
   puff pastry,
1.5 kg of spinach,
4 anchovy fillets,
50 g of butter.

*Preparation time:*
15 minutes.

*cooking time:*
35 minutes.

**Q**UICKLY blanch the fresh spinach. Chop it roughly, and heat them in butter for a few minutes. Season with salt and better.
In a pie plate (ideally made of cast-iron as it guarantees an even and quicker baking), set the thinly rolled out pastry.

Fill it with spinach, and top with the anchovy fillets in oil, 2 or 3 knobs of butter and bake in a hot oven for 20 minutes.

Instead of using anchovy fillets, you can poêlé fresh sardines with a little olive oil.

# Coulis de tomates fraîches

2 kg of tomatoes,
1 onion,
3 garlic cloves,
4 tablespoons
   of olive oil,
1 tablespoon
   of caster sugar,
1 tablespoon
   of tomato concentré,
salt and pepper,
basil or tarragon leaves,
3 twigs of parsley,
1 twig of thyme,
1 bay leaf,
25 cl of chicken stock.

PEEL and mince the onion. Take the tomatoes, remove their stalks, and blanch them to peel them more easily.

Cool them in chilled water to stop the cooking process. Chop the tomatoes, and remove the seeds and the pulp.

In a stewpot, brown the whole garlic cloves (skinned) in olive oil. Add the minced onion and sweat it slightly. It should not brown.

Then add in the peeled and seeded tomatoes, the tomato concentré, the chicken stock, and season with salt, pepper, caster sugar, parsley, thyme, bay leaf, and eventually a few leaves of tarragon or basil.

Simmer for 40 minutes.

# Tomates-cerises sautées à la ciboulette

## SAUTÉ CHERRY TOMATOES AND CHIVES

*For 4 :*

1 kg cherry tomatoes,
50 g of butter,
25 g of shallot,
one bunch of chives,
salt and pepper.

TAKE the tomatoes, remove the stalks, poach them in boiling water for 30 seconds, and cool them in chilled water. Peel them.

Sauté them in butter with a pinch of minced shallots and chives. Season slightly with salt and pepper.

You may add a hint of garlic before you serve.

# *Tomates farcies*

## STUFFED TOMATOES

1 kg of tomatoes,
salt and pepper,
olive oil,
500 g of cultivated
   mushrooms,
400 g of ham,
150 g of the white part
   of a bread,
100 g of grated
   Parmesan cheese.

TAKE middle-sized tomatoes and cut their stalk and the top part of the tomato off. Slightly squeeze the juice and the seeds out.

Sprinkle the inside of the tomatoes with salt and pepper, and a dash of olive oil. Set them on an oiled baking tray.

Mince the mushrooms, the ham, some white part of a bread together, add a hint of garlic, and season with salt and pepper.

Stuff the tomatoes and sprinkle with breadcrumbs and grated Parmesan cheese, as well as a little olive oil.

Bake in the oven for 14 to 16 minutes.

# Tagliatelles aux tomates et aubergines à la cardamome

## TAGLIATELLE WITH TOMATO, AUBERGINES AND CARDAMOM SAUCE

*For 4 :*

400 g of tagliatelle,
2 fine ripe tomatoes,
2 aubergines/eggplants,
10 g of ground
   cardamom,
olive oil.

Take the tomatoes, remove the stalks, poach them in boiling water for 30 seconds, and cool them in chilled water. The skin should now come off easily. Cut the tomatoes lengthways, and remove the pulp and the seeds.

Cut the aubergines stalks off, wrap the aubergines in foil and bake them for 30 minutes, or until the flesh is soft and can be removed easily with a spoon.
Mix the flesh with olive oil until the purée is soft, and season with salt and pepper. Add in the cardamom, and stir.

Cook the tagliatelle in 2 l of salted boiling water for 5 to 10 minutes according to whether they are fresh or not, strain, and set the pasta in a bowl, and mix with the aubergine caviar and the finely diced tomatoes.

# Farfalles aux fonds d'artichauts, fèves et pointes d'asperges

## FARFALLE WITH ARTICHOKE HEARTS, BROAD BEANS, AND ASPARAGUS TIPS

**For 4 :**

400 g of farfalle,
4 small purple
   artichokes,
16 asparagus tips,
500 g of broad beans,
half a bay leaf,
a twig of thyme,
2 tablespoons
   of olive oil,
3 tablespoons
   of white wine,
salt and pepper.

REMOVE the leaves and the chokes of the artichokes so as to keep the hearts and their stalks (keep 3 cm). Divide each of the hearts in 4. Brown them in a thick saucepan with olive oil, and water with 3 tablespoons of white wine.
Cover the artichokes with water. Add the bay leaf, and the twig of thyme. Leave to simmer until all the liquid evaporates. Put to one side.

Poach the asparagus tips in salted water for 10 minutes. Cool them with chilled water, so as to stop the cooking process. Shell the broad beans and remove their skin. Poach them in salted boiling water as well for 4 minutes and cool them with chilled water.

Melt a little butter in a saucepan, brown the asparagus tips, the artichokes and the beans. Cook the farfalle in 2 l of salted boiling water for 2 minutes, strain, and mix with the beans, artichokes and asparagus tips.

# Spaghettis au fenouil safrané

## SPAGHETTI AND FENNEL WITH SAFFRON

*For 4 :*

400 g of spaghetti,
3 fennel heads,
1 pinch of saffron,
3 fruits of star anise,
olive oil,
a tablespoon of pastis,
1/2 l of chicken stock,
salt and pepper.

CLEAN the fennel and chop it into small squares or bevels. Brown the fennel in olive oil for 2 minutes, then water with the chicken stock.

Add a pinch of saffron, the anise and leave to simmer for 15 minutes. The fennel should still be crisp.

Cook the spaghettis in 2 l of salted boiling water for 10 minutes, then strain and mix with the fennel.

# Spaghettis aux trois céréales, aux chanterelles et aux olives

## SPAGHETTI WITH CHANTERELLES AND OLIVES

*For 4 :*

400 g of spaghettis,
   preferably the three
   cereals kind,
400 g of chanterelles,
20 green olives,
a tablespoon
   of chicken stock,
20 g of butter,
chives,
salt and pepper.

CLEAN the chanterelles. Sauté them in very hot oil so that they release their water, strain and keep them warm.

Blanch the green olives twice for 3 minutes. Stone both the green and the black olives, and divide them into two, lengthways.

Sauté the chanterelles in butter, then add the olives, a tablespoon of chicken stock, and 10 g of butter.

Cook the pasta in 2 l of salted boiling water for 10 minutes, strain them, and mix in a salad bowl with the chanterelles and the olives. Stir and serve immediately.

# Spaghettis au blé complet et au pistou

## WHOLEWHEAT SPAGHETTI AND PESTO SAUCE

*For 4 :*

400 g of wholewheat
  spaghetti,
1 garlic clove,
15 basil leaves,
5 tablespoons
  of olive oil,
2 tomatoes,
50 g of pine nuts,
100 g of finely
  grated cheese,
salt and pepper.

TAKE the tomatoes, remove the stalks, and blanch the tomatoes to remove their skin. Cool them in chilled water to stop the cooking process.

Divide the tomatoes into 2 lengthways to remove the pulp and seeds. Dice the flesh finely.

Peel and crush the garlic clove, mince it together with basil leaves and pine nuts.

Add in the olive oil and the tomato dice. Cook the spaghetti in salted boiling water for 10 minutes. Strain them, and mix in a salad bowl with the pistou.

Serve, and top with grated Parmesan cheese.

# Riz aux endives, à la badiane et à l'orange

## RICE WITH CHICORY, STAR ANISE, AND ORANGE

*For 4 :*

200 g of Basmati rice,
3 tablespoons
   of olive oil,
20 cl of water,
30 cl of orange juice,
2 chicory heads,
star anise,
50 g of butter.

CLEAN the chicory, and cut it into 1 cm thick slices. Express 30 cl of orange juice. Heat 3 tablespoons of olive oil in a casserole, and throw 200 g of basmati in it. Stir until the rice changes to a translucent colour.

Pour in the water and the orange juice, add the chicory and the anise, and leave to simmer for 15 minutes until the rice absorbs the liquid.

Add 50 g of butter and stir with a fork. Remove the anise and serve immediately.

**You may also use this recipe for a salad :** in that case, do not cook the chicory, leave the rice to cool down, and serve the raw chicory and the rice with a dressing.

*Write down your own suggestions and culinary secrets on this page...*

*and on this one...*

 *...and end on this one.*

Achevé d'imprimer
sur les presses de l'imprimerie Grafiche Zanini,
Bologna, Italia,  mai 2000.